Jacky Newcomb is the UK's leading expert on the afterlife, having dedicated her life to the subject. She is a *Sunday Times* bestselling author with numerous awards to her name, a regular columnist for *Take a Break*'s *Fate & Fortune* magazine, and is a regular on ITV's *This Morning*, Lorraine Kelly's show and C5's *Live with Gabby*.

Also by Jacky Newcomb:

Messages from Angels

Messages from Angels

Real signs our loved ones are looking down

Jacky Newcomb

Harper True Fate

A few details have been changed to protect the privacy of the individuals concerned.

HarperTrueFate
An imprint of HarperCollins*Publishers*
77–85 Fulham Palace Road,
Hammersmith, London W6 8JB

www.harpertrue.com
www.harpercollins.co.uk

First published by HarperTrueFate 2014

1 3 5 7 9 10 8 6 4 2

A catalogue record of this book is available from the British Library

PB ISBN: 978-0-00-810506-8
EB ISBN: 978-0-00-758391-1

Prologue

People have spoken of angelic encounters for millennia. They occupy the area of the light-spectrum that we don't normally see. There are layers of hidden worlds that sometimes cross our own and just occasionally, almost magically, interact in a way we can experience.

Is life as straightforward as we imagine it? Is what we see with our physical eyes all there is to life? No, of course not. The trouble is that our human eyes can only view such a small amount of 'what is'. So much of what is 'out there' we cannot see, and yet we are able to make use of these energies. Infrared, ultra-violet, X-rays, radio waves; we can't see them but we can scientifically measure them. When I say we can't 'see' them, of course there are always occasions when humans have seen and experienced that which sits outside the visible spectrum; and when we can't see we might still be able to sense, touch and smell those spaces beyond our normal waking experience.

There have always been reports of angelic visions and contact from the spirits of the deceased; our own loving angels, reaching out from heaven to the earth side of life ... We call them miracles.

I've been fascinated by angel experiences for as long as I can remember. My own experiences and those of my readers have now filled many volumes. I love the way these magical encounters interact with our own everyday lives, appearing as they do in the most unexpected and often unexplained ways. I began writing my angel-experiences books after doing research to explain the mysterious phenomenon that had been part of my own life. Crossing several generations, we seemed open to the phenomena. My grandmother had psychic encounters, both my mum and dad and now my sisters, daughters, nieces and nephews and even my granddaughter have been witness to spiritual encounters. As time went on we would share our visitations from long-dead relatives or mini miracle-like angelic interactions.

I realised that just as we were comforted by sharing these personal afterlife encounters, others might benefit from hearing about them too. The more stories I shared the more readers responded by confiding their own supernatural interactions. As well as being comforting they were surely enlightening; they bring wonder and a sort of realisation that enchantment is all around. Our whole existence contains concealed aspects that we only rarely get to glimpse. Some things that happen in life appear predestined or pre-planned, others almost appear as lessons we have to work our way through, and it's at these times that contact from the other side seems stronger.

Sometimes these encounters are subtle, but other times their complexity and genius is mind-blowing. When I publish a story, I usually find another very similar encounter to print right alongside it. Sometimes there are so many stories in my files it is difficult to know which to opt for and which to leave behind. I must confide that for every story I select I have probably rejected another ten that were perfectly viable but were just a little too similar. That in itself is amazing. So many unrelated people all over the world receiving signs from their angels!

While we may encounter one or two of these experiences within a lifetime, they are common when spread among the whole population. We all have those 'What happened there?' moments or our 'How did that happen?' or 'Did that just happen?' times! These are the experiences that I have chosen for you here.

Let's explore a little …

Chapter 1

Signs from my Angels

I remember when my stepdad, Brian, was eighty-nine and in hospital with a kidney infection. The infection made him muddled and confused where normally he was very lucid and aware. One day when Mum went in to visit he told her about the man in the bed opposite him. The strange tale went something like this: '... and his visitors had squirrels on leads!' Huh? Squirrels on leads? Yes, he was very muddled indeed! My mum explained carefully and kindly, 'No, Brian, the medicine is muddling you up. Think about it. Why would squirrels be allowed in a hospital?' To him the encounter was very real. Was it a hallucination or something else?

On the next visit he was still mixed up. 'The fire alarms went off in the hospital and we were all evacuated!' he explained excitedly. In his confused state he 'recalled' the entire episode. 'Me and the man opposite, we climbed out of a window and got a taxi!' Yet here was a seriously ill man who'd spent the last couple of years in a wheelchair. He couldn't walk, but in his mind he'd managed to find the money for a taxi in his pyjama pocket and made his escape by climbing out of a window. He explained it in great detail, but it hadn't happened, of course. It was confusion due to the infection. I'd like to add an extra note here: people who are close to death often have out-of-body experiences (and sometimes people have them for no apparent reason, so don't get worried if you have had them too). Maybe it was possible that Brian *had* left the hospital – but it wasn't in his physical body.

Our lovely man recovered, but not for long. Shortly after the following New Year, now aged ninety, he was rushed into hospital again. Mum called me in the middle of the night and my husband and I jumped in the car, collected Mum and followed the ambulance to the hospital. This time we were told he was dying and Mum and I sat on each side of the bed holding his hand. It was very peaceful; his breathing just became shallower.

Within an hour I could see the outline of a woman standing at the end of the bed. Although I'm not normally clairvoyant in this way it was clear to me that his first wife had come to collect him and take him 'home'. Despite my own grief I was pleased for him. Then about two hours later he was moved to a side ward. I was stunned to see a bright white shape appear over the top of the privacy curtain – it floated right over the top of the bed. Was it an angel? I know that it was.

As if that wasn't enough, we were stunned at what happened next. In the early hours of the morning the hospital fire alarms started blaring out – this time for real. The nurse who'd been hovering close by rushed off to check but within five minutes she was back. I believe the fire brigade were normally called automatically in these cases – a dramatic backdrop to our grief – but nothing had been found to be wrong. The nurse muttered something about 'burnt toast' and that was that. We knew differently. Was it a coincidence? If you like! But to us it seemed to show that Brian was still lucid and his spirit still around as he slipped slowly from his body. Passing away to the sound of the fire alarms seemed like a final trumpet; something fitting and regal, or maybe just something very silly to make us laugh at a very sad time! On the last occasion he'd imagined the fire alarms, yet this time it had really happened. It was one of those weird coincidences that surround such events.

Six years earlier, when my own dad, Ron, passed away, we were bombarded with symbols of his presence from the other side. Smoke alarms went off, doorbells rang with no one there and Dad appeared in lucid dream-visitation experiences to all of his family. On the day of his passing, Mum walked into the house and the bedside alarm was ringing out – yet no one had set it (and there was no reason why it should be ringing at night). We all believed Dad was letting us know he was okay and, more importantly, that he was still around. There were so many experiences that they filled a whole book (*Call Me When You Get to Heaven*, which I co-wrote with my sister, Madeline Richardson).

Now it was Brian's turn. This lovely man – my mum's companion of the last two years – passed away later that day. His extended family all travelled to Mum's apartment and we were sitting around chatting and drinking 'a glass of something' in his honour. Then it happened. 'What's that ringing? Is it your phone?' someone asked. My husband John started walking round the apartment looking for the mystery sound. Moments later John walked back from the spare room with the bedside alarm clock in his hands. He'd tracked down the source of the mysterious ringing. Yes, you've got it: another alarm clock, several years after an alarm clock had rung on the day of Dad's passing, and one that hadn't been used for several weeks. Like Dad before him, Brian seemed to be signalling, in his humorous way, that he too was safe after passing on.

I like to think that they were both sat with us as we wished Brian 'au revoir' on this side of life, and that his spirit family were welcoming him home on the other side. Two men who had loved the same woman but had never met in life were now having a giggle on the other side … at our expense!

The soul 'recovers' on the heaven side of life. When loved ones appear in several dream-visits they look better and fitter each time they appear. Grey hair is often bright with colour, glasses and false teeth are no longer needed and wheelchairs and walking sticks are soon discarded. Other experiences over the years have shown me that, in time, the spirit appears not just fitter than when the person passed over; they appear whole. Those with missing limbs have them back again; people with thinning hair have a glowing crown-full. Children can also appear to 'grow up' if they choose; the average age of a 'spirit' person seems to be around thirty, when many on earth felt in their prime. They show themselves to us however they wish. If you're lucky enough to ever have a visit, your loved one may appear in the jumper you bought them for Christmas or their best evening gown! The spirit dream-visit seems real, because it is.

At Brian's funeral we met another relative. She told us that she'd had a strange dream too. Brian had appeared to her while she slept and said goodbye. She woke up to the sound of the house phone ringing. It was a call from a family member to say Brian had just died for real! Again, his visit was lucid. He'd actually come to say goodbye personally from the other side. Was this another strange coincidence? Of course, you start to see how these things stack-up, the evidence falling into place.

Why do the deceased visit some people and not others, you may ask. My late father explained this to me in a dream once; it depends on the person's depth of sleep. The visits are more likely to happen during the usual dream-sleep part of the cycle, especially if you've already had enough sleep. My husband has never recalled a spirit visitation of this type, strangely, but my sisters and I have them all the time. If you want the deceased to visit you in dreams then the best thing to do is wait until you have a day off work, set your alarm clock in the morning and when you wake up ask them to call (just chat normally in your mind), then go back to sleep. Try this a few times – I bet you'll be successful eventually. Of course, do write and let me know how you get on!

After the funeral a few days later still, I was sitting at my computer when I thought I heard Brian call out my name. It happened so quickly that I guessed I'd probably imagined it and didn't really think any more about it. I didn't mention it to anyone. That afternoon at Mum's apartment, Brian's daughter told us that she'd been in the kitchen earlier and she thought she'd heard her dad call her name. Mum, who was listening, said, 'Oh, me too!' Now seemed a good time to share the fact that I'd had a similar experience – he'd learned a new trick and had tried it out several times to see if it worked! So that was three of us (that we knew of), unaware of each other's experiences, but all of us heard his voice call our name … from heaven, no less! Clever, isn't it?

What I love about these experiences is that many people want to write them off as wishful thinking (as I've often done myself), but when you combine them all together you realise they mean something. I've spent many years now not just documenting my own family contact, but also sharing those of my readers. People all over the world are experiencing spontaneous afterlife contact and clever communication signs from heaven. Life continues after death and the 'deceased' can't wait to tell us all about it!

Brian, like my dad Ron, loved his earthly family very much. They were both very loving men, with lots of friends. But like us all, they were both scared of dying. Brian visited my sister Debbie one day after he'd passed on. She was sitting at home when she heard his voice quite clearly in her mind. They'd connected telepathically between one realm and the next. He told her: 'I don't know what I was so worried about, it was easy!' He was talking about his transition to heaven, and this is why I've devoted my career to sharing these amazing stories. Many people have been lucky enough to experience afterlife contact, but many more haven't. Contact like this brings comfort and joy; my life mission is to tell you all about them. Here are a few more experiences for you.

Let's start with Brenda's. It seems a little like my own. 'When my mother passed away,' she explained, 'all the family were with her in the hospital. As she slipped away I noticed a cloud shape start to form at the end of the bed. It floated up along the bed and as it reached where I was standing I noticed the cloud seemed to have a wing. Across the top was the brightest white light I have ever seen. It appeared to be sparkling, but even though it was so bright it didn't hurt my eyes. I think about this often and I am comforted to know that an angel came to take her home.' Over the years I'd hear a lot of similar stories, especially from nurses and care workers who spend a lot of time with the dying. They'd tell me how they watched the spirit of the deceased lift up, out of the physical body, or how sometimes the dying person would sit up in bed (when previously they had been too ill to move) and talk to long-dead relatives or angels who'd come to collect them and take them home. I find it so reassuring.

I was fascinated by Elaine's letter and knew you would love to read it too. 'Hi Jacky, I lost my mum twelve years ago after a short illness,' she wrote. 'She was just fifty-nine years old. During the week leading up to her funeral I kept her little suitcase and handbag at the foot of my bed. It had many of her personal things inside, including her wedding album, which contained precious photographs of family members who had also passed over. It was a prized item.

'One night, I was in a deep sleep but woke suddenly to the noise of the wedding album being flicked through. It sounded like the rustling of the fine tissue paper that lined the album. Almost as quickly as I had awoken I fell back to sleep. Then, while I slept, my mum came to me in a dream-visit and I heard her speak. She said she was sorry she hadn't "made it", and she told me to make sure I looked after myself. It was a lovely experience.

'Mum had made a pact with her brother that if she died before him he was to look after me. After Mum left us I was an adult and married, but my uncle still kept his word. One night, the strangest thing happened. My daughter's phone rang my house at ten to four in the morning, and when I asked her what was the matter, she told me she hadn't called. Two days later, at five in the morning, my house alarm went off for no reason, and then on the Saturday my uncle passed away. I do believe it was Mum's way of letting me know she was coming to collect her brother. Your books have brought a lot of comfort to me; thank you for all the fascinating stories you share.'

It's letters like these that make the work I do worthwhile. Sometimes when people write to me it's because they have found my details on the internet. At first they may be unaware that many thousands (probably millions) of people have experienced similar phenomena to them. The internet can be a wonderful thing. It brings people together and helps us to source information that can bring us great joy and understanding. I hope people enjoy these afterlife encounters and that we are evolved enough to no longer be frightened by love crossing from one dimension to another.

Chapter 2

Feathers and Other Gifts from Our Angels

You may have heard that white feathers are said to be the calling cards of the angels, but my postbag contains many stories from readers who find white feathers after asking for a sign that their deceased loved ones are around them too. I love these simple and gentle experiences. Who would have thought that something like a feather could change someone's life?

Birds appear in most places on earth, therefore feathers appear in most places too. Are these feathers, then, from the wings of angels? I doubt it! Angels in the traditional sense are beings of light; they don't have or need wings. Birds on the other hand do need wings, and feathers are plentiful in our dimension. If I were an angel or a spirit, I would use a feather too. It's the perfect sign. It's readily available, light and easy to move around, and you can find them almost everywhere – what could be better? To be a sign from an angel, however, it usually has to have a special story. Maybe you asked for a sign or needed one.

Joanne, from England, got in touch after reading one of my books. In her story the feather signs were subtle at first, but then the experiences became more obvious. This is normal – the spirits don't want to frighten us. 'Your real-life stories helped me when Mam passed away,' Joanne wrote. 'After she died I started to see white feathers, but they weren't always in unusual places. The first three I found on the footpath; I was sceptical that these were my sign, so I tested your theory and asked for another sign, which was one of Mam's favourite flowers – a rose. The flower quickly appeared on a TV advert, but that seemed too easy again, so this time I asked for something else. I was more specific in my request and asked for an "angel" as my sign. It was quite a personal request as Mam used to collect angel ornaments, so it was something which was important to her. Bizarrely, the next TV advert that came on had an angel on it! I couldn't believe it.' Joanne's signs were just the start, and other experiences soon followed.

'The most unusual feather story I have to share was when my husband was due to go into hospital for a heart operation. We were all frightened and I asked the angels and my mam for a sign that everything would be okay. I just thought that if I knew everything was going to be okay I would cope better. I went up to make the bed and I immediately noticed a white feather on my husband's pillow. I was really pleased with this and I decided to keep the feather, wondering if this was my sign. Strangely, while I'd been making the bed, a letter had dropped through the letterbox. It was my husband's appointment letter from the hospital. What were the chances of that happening at the exact same time? I was comforted, feeling I'd got my sign. I knew the angels and Mam were telling me that my husband would be fine. Incidentally, the operation went perfectly and he is now recovering nicely.'

Wasn't it strange that Joanne found the feather just as the letter dropped on the mat? It's these little details – or, as some might call them, 'coincidences' – that make the experiences special.

Stephanie is also from the UK and she too found a feather sign. She explained: 'One day, as I was driving to pick my children up from school, I took advantage of being alone in the peace and quiet to talk to the angels. Because no one was with me I felt happy to ask out loud for the angels to show me they were listening. When I arrived at school I got out of the car and as I stepped onto the pavement, something flapped against my face. It felt like a bird's wing and I flinched, but when I looked round there was no sign of a bird. I dismissed it and carried on walking to school. A bit further on I saw a friend who immediately burst out laughing at me. She pointed to my head and asked me if I realised I had a white feather sticking out of my hair! A single white feather was lodged upright on the top of my head! I had to smile to myself at this funny sign, and I put the feather into my handbag to keep.' It seems someone's angel has a sense of humour! Also, this wasn't a frightening experience, which is always good.

Stephanie had another angel experience to share. 'My mum has a story about when she asked my brother's guardian angel to look after him while he was on a cycling holiday in France,' she told me. 'When he got home he told us how one day he'd had an urge to stop and explore a church that he was passing. When he got his photographs printed, the picture his friend had taken of him in the churchyard showed a white triangle of light shining over him. Without him knowing that my mum had been thinking of his guardian angel, he said, "Look, Mum, that must be my guardian angel watching over me."' Isn't that a fabulous experience?

It's always okay to ask the angels to help and take care of others. We can't interfere in another person's life choices, but the angels will always do what they can when it's appropriate for that person's life path. If you're worried about a loved one on this side of life, or the other side, you can always ask the angels to help them. Try it! You might get a sign too.

Some of my Facebook followers have shared their own feather experiences with me, and given me permission to tell you. I thank them all for opening themselves up in this way. One of them is Suzy. After she lost her soul mate, Tom, she was in a really bad way, naturally. A friend came round one day to accompany her on a dog walk (Tom had bought the dog for her – Suzy still has her and tells me she is a lifesaver). This friend immediately spotted a white speck on Suzy's dark-brown carpet. There were no windows open at the time, and Suzy was certain it hadn't been there earlier; if it had been she would surely have picked it up. When she crouched down to take a look she realised it was a small white feather. It's so precious to Suzy that she keeps it in Tom's picture frame.

I had a funny feather experience of my own actually, just yesterday. It might well be those humorous angels at work again. I was walking around and something was very itchy in my trousers. To be perfectly honest with you, it was getting a bit embarrassing that I was constantly scratching at myself. I did stick my hands down my trousers (discreetly, of course), but found nothing. Then this morning I was tidying up my clothes and picked up the trousers, only to notice something white inside. Yes, you guessed it – it was a small white feather! Now that is the funniest place I have ever found one, but I guess it is my own fault. I had been writing about feather experiences and asked my own guardian angel for another sign that I could share with you – I just didn't expect that. Funny is good, though.

Dot's experience shows just how persistent these signs can be. 'About two months after my mum passed away,' she told me, 'I went to London with my friend, who was terminally ill. She was in the bathroom and I was in the bedroom when I noticed a small fluffy white feather on the floor. I picked it up and put it in the bin, not really thinking about it. My friend came out of the bathroom and asked if I was okay, and when I said I was she went back in. Then I noticed the feather was on the floor again, so I put it back in the bin. This happened a few times! Then my friend came out of the bathroom again and said, "Your mum is here with us" – she just felt her around. Sadly my friend passed away a few months later and I've not seen any more feathers since.' I'm sure Dot's friend will have met up with her mother too. Spirits often do that and sometimes come back to let us know.

Sometimes people who are terminally ill or close to death become more psychic; it's almost as if they have one foot in heaven and one on earth. It's quite common for the dying or sick to see, hear and sense those that have passed on before. A feather is always a great back-up sign.

I remember when I first heard about angel feathers myself. That day I asked my own angels for a feather sign. Later, Mum and I walked into a store and there was a massive drift of white feathers. It looked like someone had opened a feather pillowcase and dropped them in our path. I was reminded of this when I read Linda's story. 'I was at the funeral of my sister's mum-in-law,' she explained, 'and as we walked away from the graveside, all these tiny white feathers came towards us. It was like we were walking through a tunnel of them. I've never seen anything like it; it was amazing.' What fun it must have been to walk through a 'cloud of feathers!'

People find such comfort in their feather signs. Sometimes the feathers answer a request for a sign, but at other times they just indicate: 'Look, I'm still around you.' Most people find white feathers, but sometimes other colours do turn up – pretty well any colour, in fact, as birds come in all colours of the visible spectrum. Actually, birds also come in colours that we can't see. Let me explain: I was watching a wildlife programme one day and they were viewing flowers through a special filter. The filter showed a pattern on a flower that couldn't be seen with the naked eye. Amazing, isn't it? Of course, the whole world must look like that – with the right pair of eyes!

Caroline told me, 'I was twenty-two and living in Ireland with my partner. I had post-natal depression and on top of that my partner was very ill. He was in and out of hospital for months, leaving me alone in the house. One day I decided to call on the angels for a sign that they were with me and that things would get better. If I'm honest, I forgot about it. The next morning, I got up for the baby as usual, made a coffee and opened the front door to look outside. As I did so there was a huge gold feather lying on the floor between the door and the frame. I was gobsmacked! I happily took this as my sign that I wasn't actually alone at all!' Now a gold feather would be pretty special. You don't get those where I live in England, although when we lived in Cornwall a neighbour kept tropical birds (I can't say I ever found any pretty coloured feathers in the garden, though, sadly).

Jessica's story made me laugh too. 'I was living in a really rough neighbourhood in the city and was desperate to move to the country,' she began. 'Being a single mum on benefits, I knew the chances of that happening were slim. One day I went to visit my friend in her gorgeous little village and saw a TO LET sign. I made a mental note to check it out online when I got home. I looked, and there was the house of my dreams, in my price range – and, best of all, the advert stated they would accept someone on benefits! I made an appointment to go and view the house the following day with my mum and three-year-old son.

'It was a gorgeous house, small but perfectly formed, with a nice big conservatory at the back. It was just two minutes from the school, village green and park. All three of us fell in love with it. Then came the surprise: as I stepped out of the front door to leave, there on the front lawn was a pure white feather. It was definitely not there when we went in.

As we left my little boy started to cry, saying he didn't want to leave his new house and wanted to bring his bed! I moved in last November and on the moving day I went up to my bedroom, opened the door, and it was full of feathers! If that wasn't a sign I'd made the right choice I don't know what is! We love it here and can't imagine being anywhere else. Thanks, angels!'

A feather is such a little thing, but it can mean such a lot. Sharon agrees. 'A few years ago I was feeling down; it was the anniversary of my mum's passing and I'd been sitting on the couch before getting up to go to another room. A few minutes later I came back and as I reached the couch there was a white feather exactly where I'd been sitting. I have no scatter cushions on the couch where it could have come from and I knew it was my mum telling me she was with me.'

Feathers don't just appear unexpectedly; sometimes they appear in fun places too. Katie had a surprise: 'I've had a few feathers since my partner died, but the latest one appeared in my bathroom, perched on my shampoo bottle! I took a picture, and it made me smile!'

I remember when we first moved to our home in Cornwall, we'd looked at stacks of houses and nothing seemed suitable. As we pulled up to this particular house I spotted a large feather stuck in the doormat. I already knew it was 'the one' before we stepped through the door. We had eighteen fantastic months in that house before moving back to the Midlands to be closer to my new granddaughter! Feathers can show you when you're on the right path, or help you to make decisions. They can guide and direct you. Most of all I think they help to confirm what you already have in your mind. Once you've already decided (or almost decided) on something, they seem to say, 'Yes, well done, this is the right thing to do. Go on, take a chance.'

At my mother's apartment building, following the recent passing of two loved ones (Mum's partner and another family friend), I get stuck with feathers every time I visit. Everyone laughs and tells me it's feathers from the pillows, but it's only me that gets them. They are mainly the tiny ones (yes, feather-pillow size, I admit), but then why do they always stick to me?

People regularly find feather signs after the loss of a loved one. Linda had already lost her father, but had recently lost her mother and brother as well when her story starts. 'My sister and I went to lay some flowers where our mum and brother's ashes were scattered,' she told me. 'Sadly, they had passed within six months of each other. I happened to sit on the little wall where they rest among the roses and said, "I wish we knew the exact spot where Dad is." Looking up, I spotted a tiny white feather wrapped up in one of the rose buds. I couldn't believe what I was seeing. I truly believe Dad was telling us, "I am here." Now we always place flowers for the three of them in the same spot.'

This symbolism comes up a lot after loss. So many bereaved people worry that they can't visit a grave or the place where ashes have been spread. But our loved ones and angels long to reassure us, 'I am here, I am wherever you are; I am with you.' Feathers are their gentle, urging sign. After passing, the spirit doesn't hang around the graveyard – well, not if we aren't there! There wouldn't be any point. If they choose to reach through the dimensions then it's because they want to see us, to visit us. They always find us. They have a sort of LOVE-GPS, a satellite navigation system that draws their energy to ours (or the other way round). Even if we've moved house, town or country, the visits still come! They always know where we are.

Have you found a feather sign from your angels or loved ones? Perhaps, like some of my readers, you could push them into the photograph frame that holds a loved one's image, or keep them all together in a pretty pot or glass jar. I like to carry a few in my purse and share them out when people are in need. It's nice to be an 'angel' too. When someone looks sad, why not be that miraculous stranger who hands over a little feather sign to let them know that angels are watching over them?

Chapter 3

Watching Over Us

Where do our loved ones go when they pass away and how do they reach out to us? A family friend died this week; his death was sudden and unexpected … to me. Actually, afterwards we realised he'd been seriously ill but had kept this information a secret. He was a proud man, like many of his generation, but by leaving his friends in the dark he'd inadvertently left us shocked as well as saddened by his death.

On the day of his passing I went to visit my mother, and I mentioned to her that I hadn't felt his spirit around us, as I had sometimes experienced with other loved ones after they had passed. It was then that I heard his voice loud and clear, but because we were talking I didn't actually hear what he said – I only recognised the very familiar accent. My husband John jokingly suggested I hit the rewind button. The voice came again, laughing this time: 'I said, I'm okay. Stop worrying about me!' I repeated what I'd heard to my mum and my husband and we were all reassured. It was exactly the way he would have said it if he'd still been alive.

So near was the voice that I was momentarily caught off-guard, and a few tears filled my eyes before I quickly pulled myself together again. What we know is that often after the physical body passes, the spirit stays close to the earth plane for a little while. From the thousands and thousands of stories people have shared with me, I have learned a lot! Sometimes spirits are curious about what we are up to on the earth plane since they left, and other times they are mesmerised as they watch their own funeral, or they just stick around to comfort the living. My comment about not feeling him around us seemed to have drawn him close. It shows how spirits are aware of our lives still, even though the physical body has passed on. Our words seem to reach the deceased on a current – and love seems to be the very method by which our sentiments travel between these dimensions.

Many stories that are sent to me revolve around spirit visitations connected to special or important occasions. They occur when we need them most. We sense them when we're sad, feel a loving hand upon a shoulder when we need their strength or are blown away by that strange flash of light in the family photo, right over the gap in the family portrait. Traditions revolve around the deceased in different countries around the world. Because people often see the spirits of the deceased in mirrors, they are sometimes covered up around the time of a passing. On other occasions an empty chair is left for the deceased (at one wake I saw the deceased, my late father-in-law, sitting in his 'empty chair').

One example is the closing of the eyes of the deceased; this began as a way of closing the 'window' from our side of life to the other. In some cultures the deceased's belongings and even the home were burnt after death in the belief that it would stop the spirit returning. Another ritual was turning family photographs face down to stop the living relatives being possessed by the deceased. Many of today's acts of respect have their roots in ancient times. Ringing bells, firing guns and wailing or chanting all come from earlier times when the noise was believed to scare away the spirits from the churchyard! I'm guessing this came about because earlier cultures also saw the spirits of the deceased, but misunderstood the reasons for their visits! These days we know they come out of love and to help us with grieving.

So where do we go after life when the physical body ends? Recently a news report told of an American man from Ohio who'd been physically dead for nearly forty-five minutes. The gentleman had experienced a heart attack, which was followed by emergency lifesaving surgery. The surgery was a success but then the man took a downward turn.

Doctors could find no pulse, no heartbeat and no blood pressure. The brain was starved of oxygen this whole time, but the resuscitation team worked on. Just as suddenly the man's heart began beating again and the man regained consciousness, with no ill effects.

The startling part of this story is the experience the man shared afterwards. During his near-death experience (NDE) he hadn't ceased to exist; he'd actually been 'somewhere'. He described walking down a 'heavenly' path, which was lined with flowers. A bright light was at the end. It was on this path that his recently deceased mother-in-law greeted him. She took his arm and steered him back down the path telling him he had to go back, it wasn't his time!

In many of the magical tales people have shared with me, heaven seems to be the place through the light at the end of the tunnel (or in this case, the path). This pathway is the link between heaven and earth. To bring us messages or signs, our loved ones need to be in this midway place or closer to the earth side of life. This between-realm is normally filled with love and loving beings.

Jenna got in touch from South Africa to tell me about a very strange experience. 'After my father passed away,' she said, 'my mother married again and had two more children, both boys. The elder of the two regularly talked about "a man in a hat" that used to watch him. Later in life my grandmother told me that my dad used to speak about a man in a hat too. The mystery spirit used to visit him as a child. Many years later, when my own daughter started asking about the man in the hat, I realised that this was more than coincidence. I wondered if this gentleman spirit was some sort of family guardian.

'When I was sixteen I fell pregnant – this is when my angel helped me the most. One night I had a very vivid dream. Someone was about to attack me, but I was saved by a man. I asked the person in my dream how I could thank him and he suggested I call my little boy Daryn. At the time, I didn't even know that I was carrying a boy. When I was thirty-two weeks pregnant I went into early labour. My baby had gone into foetal distress. I lay in the most agonising pain for the entire day but because it wasn't a normal labour, there were no contractions, and the staff at the hospital seemed unaware of the danger I was in.

'A number of times I felt myself lifting from my body; at the time I thought it was the angels sparing me from the pain. The hospital staff just seemed to ignore me for hours and hours, but then I became aware of a man standing at the edge of my bed reading the heart-monitor notes. He was dressed as a doctor and I clearly noticed a name badge on him that read Dr Quin. He was very handsome and smiled at me before shouting and making a lot of noise for the nurses to spring into action. I remember him telling them I should have been taken in for an emergency Caesarean section many hours earlier. He told them to hurry or my baby was going to die and take me with him.

'The next thing I recall is being asked to sign a consent form for the C-section. Once they realised I was underage my mother had to rush in to do it for me, all the while delaying the operation. The baby – a boy – was very poorly when he was born but recovered really quickly. I took him home four days later; he didn't even need one night in an incubator, which was startling considering what he'd been through.

'It was three days earlier that I realised something was amiss. The day after my son was born I asked to see the doctor because I wanted to thank him. This is where it gets really strange. No one knew who the doctor was. Of course, I remember the doctor's name badge, but I was told that not only was there no Dr Quin, there was no member of staff in the whole hospital with a name beginning with Q! After all this time, I have to believe the doctor was an angel in disguise! Oh, and my son is now a strapping thirteen-year-old!'

Where did Jenna's mystery stranger come from? Is this the same man appearing over and over again to different generations of the same family, or is it merely a coincidence? Jenna's family continued to have psychic experiences over the years, and here she relays another memory. 'My daughter was born five years after my son. My daughter was just a baby who had only recently started stringing sentences together when we went one day to the cemetery to lay flowers for my father. My brother was holding her and all of a sudden she piped up, "Wow, look at all the people," at the same time swinging her head from side to side, looking all around her. This seems a very normal thing to hear a child say, except for the fact that we were entirely alone in the graveyard – not one other person was there. It was amusing to see my brother's face. I thought he might fall down from fright, and he very quickly handed my daughter back to me.'

I just love the way that the children *are* the signs in some of these stories. Children see the spirits and tell the adults; the children become the messengers (or the mediums). I wonder why that is. Is it, as some people believe, that they have so recently come from the spirit realms themselves, or maybe, as another theory states, because children may see a wider spectrum of light than adults do?

Another reader, I'll call Jane, received her angel sign in a most unexpected way. 'I had been with my ex-husband for eight years and lived with him for seven years,' she told me. 'Our relationship was a violent one; he was a very abusive man. I'd wanted to leave him for a very long time but I was simply not strong enough emotionally to do it. My biggest fear (following his constant threats) was that he would take the children away.

'Then, one day, I decided to speak with my angels. I didn't ask them for anything specific, just any sign that they were watching over me. Later that day I went into a local charity shop; the manager knew me as a regular customer, but this day was a little different. For no obvious reason, she said to me, "I have something for you," and disappeared off to get it. She walked back out into the shop holding two small fabric angels, and when I offered money for them she refused. They were a gift. I was blown away. There was no way she could have known I'd asked for an angel sign that morning, and she had never given me anything like this before. I couldn't believe the coincidence of it all.

'The whole experience brought me great comfort and confidence. The angels must have heard me that night, and I was shocked at how quickly the sign came – and from somewhere I never expected! It helped to give me the courage I'd been seeking, and I finally left my abusive partner.'

... Angels from the angels? Well, why not? These little gifts were probably worth very little in monetary terms, but to Jane they were worth everything in the world – priceless, in fact.

* * *

Angels have been known to intervene to help protect someone on more than one occasion – just as they did when Sarah's son was in danger. Sarah and her family had just moved house when strange things began to happen. 'Around nine years ago,' she explained, 'my husband Dave and I moved to our dream home with our children. It was a lovely old farmhouse. Parts of it were very old and it was surrounded by huge gardens. Our eldest son left home shortly after we moved, which left just three of us: my husband, our son Len and me. Len was still attending college when we first moved in – it was a long drive to college each day, but apart from that life was great and we loved our new home.

'Then Len left college and seemed to withdraw into himself. I assumed it was just an age thing. He couldn't make up his mind if he was going to look for work or attend another college, and he seemed reluctant to talk about it. In the September he turned seventeen and to stop him feeling so isolated we decided to pay for driving lessons as a gift. He seemed quite upbeat about it at first and realised how it would help him to stay in contact with his close friends. After his first lesson I remember having this awful feeling in my stomach – I kept thinking something was going to happen. I'd been anxious when our eldest child was learning to drive, but nothing like this. I even hoped he'd come home and tell us he hated it and didn't want to carry on with the lessons, but he seemed quite pleased and wanted to carry on with them.

'By Christmas he'd had a few lessons, but by now my anxiety level was through the roof. I just kept thinking that something wasn't right. At the same time, we started experiencing odd things happening in the house. It only happened when Len and I were about. One day I was cleaning when I heard someone whisper in my ear. I jumped back in panic. It freaked me out at the time.

'Then the TV started switching itself on and off, despite the remote control being sat on top of the TV. It was as if someone or something was trying to get our attention. One day Len had things thrown at his head, and some of his belongings moved around in his bedroom. One morning his bedroom door was locked from the inside and another day I was relaxing in a warm bath when all of a sudden the cold tap just turned on by itself. When I was home alone I'd hear footsteps and whispering upstairs. I could feel the hairs on the back of my neck stand up. Len was getting more anxious too – he could also hear voices, footsteps and other weird things.

'One night I had a dream about my grandma, who had passed away a couple of years earlier – it was so vivid. She was trying to shake me and tell me something was going to happen to Len. I immediately felt that she had been instrumental in creating the other phenomena. The next moment I was awoken by a rumbling sound. The bed was moving up and down, almost as if someone was shaking it. I was terrified and I straight away thought that it must be to do with my son's driving lessons, but nothing else happened that day.

'A week before Christmas, I remember, I'd written all of my Christmas cards, and instead of posting them as we used to, we decided to deliver all the local ones ourselves. It was a chilly evening as we set out and we'd left Len at home alone – he didn't want to come with us and at the time we didn't really think anything of it. Yet when we were out, my stomach was knotted with fear again and I was so relieved to get home. The first thing I did was to call out to our son to see if he wanted a cup of tea, but there was no answer. The house seemed deathly quiet. Even our lovely dog just sat with a sad look on his face.

'My son's bedroom light was on but he wasn't there. Dave and I searched the grounds around the house and the old barns. It was then that we noticed my car was missing. Now I was terrified, remembering the dream warning.

'We rang Len's friends to see if they had seen him; they hadn't. We decided to take immediate action – Dave and I made the decision to ring the police right away. My son had taken my car and driven it to an isolated spot. Shockingly, he had tried to take his own life and he'd written us a letter to explain. The police found him during his attempt and thankfully he survived.

'What we hadn't known was that he'd been severely depressed for a long time. He was upset because of his weight, and the bullying he'd received at college had pushed him over the edge. Afterwards he was offered a lot of professional help and we watched him very closely for a long time.

'That wasn't the end of our story, though, as shortly after we'd recovered from the shock two more things happened. I was asleep one night and my grandma came to me – this time she was with her mother, my great-grandmother. The dream-visitation was in colour and Grandma was wearing a greyish suit and carrying a brown suitcase. She told me she was leaving now, and with that she and my great-grandmother turned around and just disappeared. This dream was also incredibly vivid – even after all these years, I can still remember every detail.

'Another day, around the same time, Len and I heard the phone ringing in Dave's office. The phone was standing on the desk and weirdly enough, although I was standing right next to it, I didn't even try to answer it. I just let the answerphone pick it up. When we played the message back, a husky voice had recorded a single word: 'Goodbye.' Len and I just stood there looking at one another, shocked! Bemused, I did a callback on the phone to see where the message had come from, but it just said the number was not recognised. We both knew who the caller was: it was Len's granddad, even though he'd passed on many years before.

'I felt that while Len was going through all of his problems, our deceased relatives were trying to help us, and that now things were "out in the open", they had done their work and it was time for them to go. Whatever it was, I am eternally grateful to them.

'Len now has a beautiful wife and a gorgeous child, and it's given him something to live for. His experiences gave him a real interest in Mediumship and he does have a real talent for it. For someone who used to hide away from people, you wouldn't believe it when you see him stand up in front of people now.'

I was really touched by Sarah's family experiences. Sometimes our angels and spirits are aware of things we may miss from this side of life. They can see slightly ahead to what is to come, or perhaps the most likely outcome based on the current set of circumstances. It's wonderful that the spirit family were able to hang around, bringing their signs and warning the family of the dangers. It doesn't seem an easy thing for them to do, though. There is always the confusion and potential fear that this contact might bring initially, even when the intention is clearly to bring loving support!

I also love the symbolism of the suitcase in the dream-visitation. It's one I've seen in other stories in the past. I doubt spirits need suitcases in heaven, but for us on the earthly side we understand the sign that a suitcase is something we pack when we go on a journey. I can only assume the family were going back 'home' through the light at the end of the tunnel.

And don't you love the telephone call from heaven? Isn't it clever? It happens more often than you might think, as this very sad story shows. Is it a 'coincidence'? You decide. 'Our daughter miscarried her baby at fourteen weeks,' this reader told me. 'I was by her side in the ambulance and stayed with her at the hospital. Afterwards, my husband came to the hospital to comfort her. After a while we went for a coffee, leaving our daughter with her partner on the ward. Then we stood outside for a few minutes to get some air. I was crying as I told my husband what had happened in the last few hours. Just then my husband's mobile phone rang, and bizarrely a small child said, "Hello, Granddad!" then hung up. We immediately called the number back but there was no answer. Then we rang to see if it had been our other grandson, aged four, or our granddaughter, aged two – but it wasn't.

'We still have no idea who this child was. We were left completely baffled, yet felt some kind of warmth and comfort from our strange little anonymous caller. Maybe it was just a wrong number. Who knows?'

* * *

Vivienne is from New Zealand. Her experience reflects one of my own. 'In the two years since my husband passed,' she told me, 'I feel he has been protecting me. I was never comfortable being on my own at night, but since he passed I have felt completely safe. Eleven weeks after his passing I was going to a medium to get a psychic reading and the bathroom light started flickering. It only stopped when I acknowledged his presence. I felt it was his way of letting me know he was around me, if I went to a psychic or not.

'He seems to bring me lots of little signs: pictures that need straightening, the dent in the bed that looks like someone has been sitting there and the scent of daffodils around the house. His most obvious presence is at night when I ask him to warm my cold knees – it was a standing joke between us, because I was always warming his cold knees after he had been working in his workshop late at night. At first it was just a warming sensation over the knees, even though my skin still felt cold. Now it's my whole legs, and they feel like there is a weight on them. It's a very comforting feeling knowing he's never far from me. I look forward to the day when I can contact my soul mate without having to use a medium.' Of course, Vivienne's partner is already visiting her without the assistance of a third party. Even when we have these experiences we tend to forget that, yes, this is them popping in to let us know they are okay!

This story was fun too. I think this relative may have been listening in! Will told me, 'My partner's dad passed away fourteen years ago. Every year on his birthday the clocks stop at my partner's house. This is strange but it's not just her home; the clocks stop at my house as well as his old home (now occupied by his two sons). When you first asked this question about clocks, Jacky, the door on an old clock that had never been opened, started opening on its own, despite being tight and well fitted!' It always makes me laugh when spirits hijack my stories this way.

Daphne emailed me to share her experiences after reading one of my books. 'About a month after my mother died my sister came to stay,' she wrote, 'and together we worked on sorting out the belongings at Mum's home. In the evening my sister and I went to a committee meeting. When we arrived back, my husband had laid out a tray ready to make a cup of tea, but without anybody being in the kitchen the kettle turned on by itself!

'On another occasion my sister and brother-in-law visited us for a few days at New Year. We had the iPod on playing music and after ten minutes it turned itself off. We put it back on and after half an hour it turned itself off again. This had never happened before and, almost three years on, it has never done it again. We said it must be Mum and Dad because they knew we were spending time together and they wanted to make their presence felt!

'My husband was a total sceptic while Mum was alive, and one day I asked her to do something when she died that would convince my husband that life does go on. A short while after she died, my husband's watch stopped working. He took it to the jeweller's to have a new battery put in, but when he got there they told him that the watch didn't have a battery – it was kinetic. They got it working again with no problem at all, and it has merrily ticked away ever since. I like to think this was Mum's sign.'

Becky went through a very bad time when her brother passed away, but she is convinced he came right back again. On the day of his funeral, she told me, her home phone started ringing. When she answered it, though, there was no one on the line. She called the number back and immediately heard her mobile phone ringing – which was locked and sitting in her handbag in the empty kitchen. It was then she realised that it had been her own mobile that had rung the house phone!

That evening, after the funeral service, Becky and her family were gathered in her brother's favourite pub to raise a glass to his memory. They left one chair empty, and as they did the toast there was a bright flash from the far side of the room and all the lights went out! Everyone felt it was him trying to say he was still there with them, and this comforts Becky a great deal.

Have you ever had a spirit visitation? I'm constantly amazed at the different ways in which they reach out to us to let us know they are still around. As well as bringing comfort, we can see how they sometimes literally save lives by warning us or hinting to us (maybe sometimes that is all they are permitted to do). It's wonderful to know that our angels care for us still.

Chapter 4

Mysteries and Magic

I'm not sure if angels sit on clouds all day as tradition dictates. Maybe they do. There are different types of angels and many of them – the guardian angels; our own personal protectors – are very close to us on the earth side of life. Their role, after all, is to take care of us, to reassure us and keep us on the right track. Their signs are usually subtle; there seems to be an unwritten rule about it. I can't imagine it would be very helpful if your angel appeared clearly in front of you and you died from shock! People say they want to see their guardian angel in front of them, but I wonder if they really mean it. I think I'd be pretty scared, myself.

Perhaps a subtle sign is safer, like the one Erica told me about. She and her husband both believe in angels and the afterlife and had been discussing the subject while sitting in the living room watching television. Suddenly they both spotted a plume of white smoke spiralling up from a vase of flowers on the table. It carried on for a few seconds and then disappeared. There were no candles lit in the room that evening, so there was no reason for this strange occurrence at all. Was it a sign that 'someone' or 'something' was listening in, or was there a more normal explanation?

Sometimes these wisps appear in photographs, especially of children. One mother wrote to me numerous times over the years to share stories about her family. She had two psychic children (and two without psychic ability). With the youngest girl the mother used to wait until she was talking to 'no one' (no one on this side of life), and rush to get her camera. The resulting photographs always had a white or green type of 'smoke' or fog next to the little girl. Strange, isn't it?

Linda wrote to tell me about what happened after her Aunt May passed on. 'When I got the phone call to say that she had died I went right over to my granny's because my mum was on holiday. We were sitting in the living room when all of a sudden this black smoke appeared in the room; it seemed to gather at Granny's feet. I'm sure it was a sign from Aunt May, letting her mum know she was okay.'

Sometimes our signs come from humans – well, at least they look like humans! Julie and her husband encountered a mysterious stranger. I'll let her explain. 'We had both been offered early retirement and had been chatting about what to do. We were on holiday at the time and had to give our answer as soon as we got back. I remember the occasion very well: my husband was reading his newspaper and I was reading a book about angels, and a man – a complete stranger – walked towards our table. I noticed he had the most stunning eyes as he leaned in towards us; even my husband commented on it. The man then spoke to us, saying, "You've worked a long time …" Then he suddenly walked away. We were both stunned. I immediately wrote down what he'd said because it seemed quite poignant. Afterwards, we looked for the man but never saw him again. Those wise words definitely helped us decide what to do!'

Was this man an angel in disguise or a heavenly human sharing messages from the other side? Who knows! I will tell you this, though: one thing occurs on a regular basis with these mysterious-strangers-who-disappear stories – they always have the most beautiful and striking eyes! People always point it out to me.

Themes from nature are common, as are dream-visits. Rachel's experience involved both. 'Last night I went to bed,' she told me, 'and in my mind I could see my late mum in a field of yellow flowers; she was smiling. The next morning I woke up and looked out the window and a yellow rose had bloomed in the garden!'

Mollie was just thirteen when she emailed me her story. 'I was in class and the teacher asked us to draw the "seven days of God's journey on creating the world" for homework. I was working on the final drawing and needed to draw God resting (my image of God) – I drew a man sitting down, leaning his back against a blossom tree with his hands and feet resting on the summer grass. For some reason I drew a pillow underneath each arm and leg and behind his head. Later I showed my mum and she was stunned. She told me Grampy (who was knocked over by a drunk driver) had died lying up against a blossom tree. Mum always wished there'd been a pillow to break his fall! I don't believe in coincidences!' Maybe Grampy took his opportunity to connect with Mollie and bring her mother the sign she'd longed for?

Children can be very aware of angels and spirits, often seeing them when adults do not. Nick knows this only too well. 'When Mum died, my brothers and I rented her flat out. We had a succession of tenants and the latest tenants moved in about eighteen months ago. They are a nice couple with a daughter, who is probably four or five. I met them before they moved in but hadn't seen them since. I noticed that the female partner had a nice energy and I sensed that she had spiritual inclinations. She said that her daughter was quite sensitive and that they picked this property because it was nice and quiet. They even decorated the property at their own expense because they wanted it newly decorated, which I didn't mind.

'They kept saying that I should come round and see the property and have a cup of tea with them sometime, but due to work commitments it was ages before I was able to take them up on their invite. Eventually I went round and met them properly. The flat was beautifully decorated, and their daughter was sleeping in Mum's bedroom. When I visited she was playing quietly in her room.

'Over tea, Claire, the female partner, said that she hoped I liked the property and the way it was decorated. I told them I approved and that if Mum was looking down on us then I was sure she would love the way they had looked after it as well.

'At that point Claire said that their daughter had been having problems sleeping because someone else had been in the bedroom and it had frightened her. Claire was open-minded about the spirit realms and I suggested she ask any spirits to leave, because I'd heard this sometimes works. As the little girl was sleeping in my mum's old room I told her I suspected it might be Mum anyway, rather than something malevolent.

'That night, when I went to bed, Mum came to me in a dream. She apologised for visiting the little girl and explained that she'd simply wanted to check that she was okay but had no idea that the little girl might be able to see her! The next morning I phoned and told Claire, and she was relieved.' Isn't it fascinating that the deceased still visit places that were important to them when they lived on earth, as well as visiting loved ones? It's almost like they're tourists!

Chapter 5

Asking for Signs

Many of the signs described in this book have been spontaneous, but asking for signs does seem to help manifest them. Thinking about the deceased, wondering if our angels are around … yes, this does help, but asking specifically for something (out loud or in your head) seems to be the key. It certainly worked for Carla. I'll let her explain. 'I'd been on holiday for two weeks and felt really relaxed and chilled out. Within a few hours of being back at work again I was back to my usual stressed-out self. All of a sudden, on the Thursday, completely out of the blue, I received an email from another firm asking if I would be interested in a job. It sounded great, but they wanted to take me on not as an employee but on a self-employed basis. Obviously this was a massive step to take, especially as I'd been employed since I left school at sixteen. After sitting down with my husband, Mark, and working out figures, I decided I had to give it a go – I handed in my notice on the Monday.

'The company I'd been working with seemed disappointed that I was leaving and my director asked me to stay. I did think long and hard about it but in the end I realised it was time for me to take my leave! I stood by my decision and continued to work out my notice, but then, as the time grew nearer, I began to have second thoughts about whether I had done the right thing. I'd really begun to panic about it. As I was doing some chores for work, wandering around the streets delivering the post, I asked my angels whether I had done the right thing. I never spoke out loud, because I felt sure the angels would be able to hear my thoughts. I decided to ask the angels for a penny as a sign that I had done the right thing, but then I thought a penny was a bit too obvious, so I changed it to a five-pound note. Five pounds would be much harder for the angels to manifest, wouldn't it?

'Two days passed and I hadn't seen my sign, so I started to feel like maybe I should have stayed where I was – but then I came into work that morning … As I opened the front door I found a folded-up five-pound note wedged underneath it! I realised right away that it had to be a sign from my angels. I am now looking forward to my new journey in life and I just know that my angels will be there to help me along the way.'

Pauline hadn't seen her father for many years due to a divorce in the family, but when she discovered he was seriously ill, she managed to visit him and make the much-needed connection once more. He didn't live much longer, as Pauline explains: 'One day he took a sudden turn for the worse. He died at 6.55 p.m., but we got there at 7 p.m. We'd missed his passing by five minutes. I was heartbroken that I hadn't been with him. Luckily, I'd been able to tell him how much I loved him and that I had never stopped loving him [before he died]. I asked if he would let me know he was okay when he got to the other side.

'He had a lovely send-off – we walked out to the tune "Always Look on the Bright Side of Life" from the Monty Python film. He loved that tune. About three months later the fire alarm began blaring out, yet there was nothing in the house that could have set it off – no smoke, no fire; the cooker wasn't even on and the alarm had never gone off before. I knew it was Dad bringing me the sign I had asked for!' These alarms are a common theme, as you can see!

Songs can also prove a useful method of communication. After saying a final goodbye and collecting her grandpa's things from the nursing home where he had lived, Vicki asked for a sign. 'I thought I would ask the angels to give me a sign that my grandpa and grandma were now together in heaven. Then straight away, within seconds, the song 'Together in Electric Dreams' by singer Philip Oakey came on the radio. The words 'We'll always be together …' were just the confirmation I needed!

Over the years I've heard it a few times and it never fails to cheer me up when I feel a little low. The song came on once when I was stood in my kitchen and as I looked out the window I noticed a rainbow in the sky. I even had it played at my wedding. I like to think Grandma and Grandpa were there to hear it.'

Bridget, one of my Facebook followers, has also shared her experiences. She told me about a difficult patch she was going through a few years ago, when she was experiencing some odd activity at her house. Pictures would repeatedly fall off the walls, and objects kept flying off the shelves. Understandably, she found this very alarming, especially as she was living on her own with a young son. It was her son, though, who gave her a clue as to what might be happening. He said he kept seeing a man in the house (although Bridget never saw anyone), and would often get quite upset about it. Eventually, Bridget got fed up of being scared and decided to try asking the angels for help. She had read a piece I'd written in a magazine explaining how to do this, so she followed my advice to relax and picture a warm glow of light surrounding you as you call upon them. After she'd done this, she thanked the angels for their protection and asked them to send her a sign to let her know that they were listening. When she woke the next morning she found a clear image of an angel on the bathroom window!

Bridget even sent me a photo of the shape and I agreed; it looked just like an angel! Wasn't that a strange one? Sometimes people send me photographs of wings on a window, but I'm afraid these are normally the outline of a bird that has been unlucky enough to hit the glass! This photograph of Bridget's was different. It looked as if the image was made up of condensation that had been pushed through an angel stencil.

Laura also asked for a sign. She told me how her father always used to do their decorating when he was alive, so when she began wallpapering her own home she asked him to give her a sign that he was helping her. She laid the length of cut wallpaper on the pasting table and left the room. When she came back to hang it on the wall she spotted a cross drawn at one end of the paper. She was stunned – that was exactly what her dad used to do when he was decorating to remind him which end of the paper was the top!

What sort of signs do you think your own loved ones and angels might leave for you? Sometimes the deceased select symbols that have meanings for you both. One of my relatives is known for her collection of china cups and saucers. When her time comes I wonder if she'll find a way of using that as her sign … Most people are known for something. For me, I guess it will be angels themselves, or perhaps the large pieces of costume jewellery I wear. Maybe my own sign will be cats. My loved ones on this side of life know how much I love them. You just know our spirit friends will use these recognised personal symbols to make their presence known.

These signs might come in many forms, as we have seen. Items can manifest out of thin air (usually small items, like coins, crystals or jewellery). These sudden spirit appearances of objects are called 'apports'. When my dad passed away I was out with a friend at a crystal warehouse. All of a sudden a tiny piece of crystal appeared in mid-air and then dropped to the floor. There were no shelves where we stood, so it made us jump!

Scents as signs are common too. Flowers, tobacco or a particular perfume brand might make an appearance. Even if a large crowd is present, the scent might only be noticed by two or three people. The scents can appear spontaneously in a closed lift or inside the car. You could be in a house with the windows closed and the scent of your mum's chocolate cake wafts by for a moment before quickly fading away. Scents, for the most part, are non-scary and lots of fun, so I like them a lot.

Alarms and bells are a common theme, as many of our stories show. Clockwork items are common too – clocks stopping and starting, clockwork toys jumping into action in the middle of the night and, in some previous stories I've come across, clockwork music boxes playing with perfect timing. In an earlier book I shared an experience of how one man, missing his mother after she had recently passed over, shouted out goodbye as he left the house. Spookily, a toy dolly jumped into life and 'spoke' in return. Of course it's possible that the change of heat in the house may have switched on the talking mechanism ... or am I clutching at straws here? Looking for a 'logical' explanation when there really isn't one?

Coincidences can be another sign. For example, you could be daydreaming, thinking about your late mother and wondering if she is okay and if she made it safely to heaven. Then, out of the blue, the TV presenter says her name several times, relating to a segment on the TV show that is playing quietly in the background. Another could be that you are chatting in your mind to your granddad, and as you do so his favourite song plays unexpectedly on the radio. Maybe the song is an old one that you haven't heard for years and years, making it even more surprising.

Our brains are created to see images, to fill in the missing gaps and make sense of what we see. When I've been driving in the car or thinking about my late father, I often see his name spelled out in car number plates, or perhaps his initials appear on the side of a business truck. I wonder if this happens more than we realise. As we've already seen, so many of these experiences seem beyond rational explanation. Let's have a look at some more stories.

Chapter 6

Always Around You

Our guardian angels and our angel loved ones are always around us. They long to show us how they are aware of what is going on in our lives.

Debbie is another of my Facebook followers who has shared her experiences with me. She once had a very memorable Mother's Day. First, her clock stopped and then she heard a buzzing in her ears, followed by her mother's voice, saying, 'I love you.' Have you ever had buzzing like that in your ears? I have, and it's often followed by some kind of psychic phenomenon ...

Gillian, from New Zealand, was greatly comforted by an extraordinary experience she had after the death of her mother. Unfortunately, she had been away for work when her mother passed, so she had to drive for several hours to see her at the funeral home. She stayed with her for nearly an hour. Eventually, Gillian hugged her and told her she had to go, as everyone would be waiting for her at home.

She rested her face against her mother's and said that if she could only give her a sign that she and her late father were together and happy it would make it easier for her to leave. As soon as she lifted her face away she saw a multicoloured aura emanating from her mother's skin. She could hardly believe what she was seeing, and tried to touch it. The rainbow colours were all over her hand, yet there was no window in the room to cause this light effect, and it had happened all of a sudden, an hour after she had arrived.

Gillian thanked her mother for the sign, told her she loved her and then left. It really did feel as though she had been given what she needed, she told me. For days afterwards she was walking on air. It was a huge relief to know that her mother was now with her dad and happy. Fourteen years on, that memory is still as clear to Gillian as it was on that day. She now knows that the place her mother has gone to is a joyful one, and that one day she'll join her there, where her loved ones will all be waiting. She only hopes that she will be able to give her own family a similar sign when that day comes.

I love rainbow signs. Val had a similar experience of them. 'On the day of my husband's funeral,' she explained, 'a beautiful rainbow appeared; it seemed to be a sign that said he was with us and it appeared to follow us around throughout the day. Last week I was feeling particularly sad. One morning, when I woke up I realised there were little "spheres" of beautiful rainbow colours all around my bedroom. They were on the walls, on the carpet and everywhere I looked. The peaceful and calm energy was amazing. I just knew it was a sign that my husband was still all around me and our family. Rainbows are now our sign from heaven – our little bridge of love.'

Anna, meanwhile, received a radio sign. 'One of the last things my mum ever said to me before she passed away was: "Don't let anything change you." One day, I was at her grave and feeling upset. As I walked back to my car, I spoke to Mum in my head, telling her: "Mum, if you can hear me, send me a sign." I was crying as I leant forward to put the radio on, but right away I noticed that the words that were playing were poignant: "Don't go changing …" the song rang out loud and clear. I still hear it a lot when I feel down.'

Julia explained that her mum gets regular visits from her dad. He lets her know he is around by coughing! Isn't that funny? If you were sitting quietly at home and you heard the sound of coughing in a room where you were sitting 'alone', I expect it would probably make most people jump! After her dad passed on, Julia herself found a red admiral butterfly and several little coins, which she took as personal signs from her dad. A little less scary, I think!

Janet is a family friend of mine who once told me, 'When I'm worried I smell my dad's tobacco and my door bell rings!' Janet's dad is a regular visitor, it seems! My own dad was a smoker. Towards the end of his life he smoked very little and when he did it was usually in secret (we all disapproved). He used to eat a lot of peppermint sweets to disguise the smell. When he came back after he'd passed on he brought with him the smell of peppermints and cigarettes mixed together. I hope he isn't smoking in heaven now!

I've had many angel and afterlife experiences of my own, as you may know. I always share them with my readers. Sometimes they go onto Twitter or Facebook, and other times they make it into my books. Recently, I had a funny feather experience and I shared it on my social networking page. I'm not sure it was related to angels, but it did make me laugh.

I had a beautiful white feather – a large fluffy one – which had arrived in the post along with a gift from a kind reader. I'd kept the feather in the cupboard for a while, but as I sometimes make things I decided I would use it in a craft of some sort. My current office is in an upstairs bedroom and my craft items are downstairs, so I placed the feather on the landing with the intention of taking it with me on my next trip down. Later that afternoon I went to pick it up and was very disappointed. My cat Tigger, a fat ginger tom, had found it first. He'd clearly enjoyed playing with it and had turned this beautiful object into a wet and soggy mess. Yes, folks, it was completely ruined. At first I was cross with him, but once he started purring and zig-zagging in and out of my legs I soon melted – naughty cat! He made me laugh, so I took a photo of the bedraggled feather and posted it on Facebook for fans to enjoy and have a giggle too.

Sometime later I had an email from Maureen, a follower of the page. 'I was on Facebook one day,' she wrote, 'reading your comments as usual, feeling very ill and with no money. I remember you commented about the angels saying they would show a sign of being around by bringing a white feather. I decided to ask for one.

'Shortly afterwards I sold some of my yellow chickens to a very smart man in a suit. He pulled out the money from his wallet. Interestingly, between two notes was a long, thin, straggly white feather, just like the one in your picture. The man said, "What's that?" He didn't know where it had come from. He went on to tell me that he had just been to a hospital as his dad was very poorly, and it was only a couple of months earlier that he'd lost his mother. I reassured him that the angels would look after him and his dad, and if he needed someone to talk to he could contact me. When he went, I went straight back to the Facebook page and compared the feather to the picture you'd posted. The man's feather was identical to the one in your photograph, so I thanked the angels for showing they were there for me, and for bringing me the money I so badly needed. I knew that the man and his dad had angels watching over them too. Thank you, Jacky!'

Isn't that funny? Who knew that my cat sucking on a feather might end up having a long-term meaning for someone I didn't even know personally? It still makes me laugh to think about it, but you have to admit, the feathers do get around a bit. Maybe the feathers don't need to be perfect to have that special meaning, either.

Here's one final story: yesterday, just as I finished working on the book for the day, I was thinking about some of the wonderful angel experiences I'd been sorting through. As I walked into the lounge I spotted something white on the floor. What was it? Of course you know!

Angels are all around us. My research over many years leaves me in no doubt that we are watched over and taken care of by a higher power. That higher power sends his angels and our deceased loved ones to keep an eye on us. In whatever way they can, they bring us signs to show us they are here.

Remember, if you want a sign too, why not ask your angels to bring you one? Thank you for reading. Let's get together again very soon.

Much love,

Jacky x

eNewsletter

Moving Memoirs

Stories of hope, courage and the power of love…

If you loved this book, then you will love our Moving Memoirs eNewsletter

Sign up to…

- Be the first to hear about new books
- Get sneak previews from your favourite authors
- Read exclusive interviews
- Be entered into our monthly prize draw to win one of our latest releases before it's even hit the shops!

Sign up at

www.moving-memoirs.com